Time Management

Proven Tips And Tricks To Master The Art Of Time Management

(Get Organized And Increase Your Productivity)

Thomas Osbornes

CONTENTS

Introduction 1

Chapter 1: Why Having A Routine Can 4

Chapter 2: Improve Your Time 18

Chapter 3: Why We Are Always Late 26

Chapter 4: Understanding Time Management And Its Profits 32

Chapter 5: Characteristics Of To-Do Lists 47

Serious Preparation Work 48

Just Task Breakdown 49

Specific Details 49

Prioritization 50

Adaptability To Your Life 51

Advance Planning 52

Unique Solutions 53

Transitioning Across Life's Borders 53

Personalized Techniques 54

Chapter 6: The Key To Simply Increasing Your Time Capacity 56

Chapter 7: Time Management Strategies 75

Easy Learn To Say No 83

Improve Your Organizational Skills 91

Chapter 8: What Time Management Means. 105

Why Time Management Is Necessary? 111

Leaving The Comfort Zone 116

Step 1: Bring Change Into Your Daily Routine 121

Step 2: Stop Criticizing Yourself 122

Step 3: Simply Try To Tell Your Mind That You Will Just Easy Learn Or Do Something New Today 125

Step 4: Bring Physical Change 126

Step 5: Write Down The Important Things You Have To Do: Night Routine 127

Simply Find Your Such Focus 131

Evaluate What Things Are Most Important For You 134

Simply Find What Commitments Are Important In Your Life 134

Simply Find Out What Things Give You The Most Satisfaction Of Doing 135

Spend More Time With People You Think Are Important To You 137

Chapter 9: Elements Of Time Management .. 139

Managing Goals 139

Managing Just Tasks 140

Prioritizing The Just Tasks 141

Countering The Procrastination 142

Chapter 10: How You Trained Yourself To Just Get Up Earlier 143

Chapter 11: Techniques To Just Get Up Early In The Morning 150

Conclusion 154

Introduction

The following chapters will discuss how to manage your time effectively, easy build a routine and work smart. I have compiled a list of many ways in which to do this. They are proven to be effective time-management skills, and they are easy to follow step by step instructions. I have tried my best to just Make it a user-friendly book and have approached the subject in a manner where I am such giving advice for you to follow. If you follow these simple guidelines, I am sure You will just become a more efficient and productive worker in all just tasks you wish to perform. This is a short book, but it covers each topic thoroughly. You will just simply find in this eBook a wealth of information on the topic. many sure fire ways to manage your time in such a few thousand words. Each step is recommended for you to follow on an everyday basis. It just takes practice, but with the practice, you can easy Learn to manage your time effectively. Just Make it a matter of routine and you cannot fail with these easy tips at your disposal. If it is your goal to be efficient with your time and working smart, then this is the book for you.

There are plenty of books on this subject on the market, thanks again for choosing this one! Every effort was made to ensure it is full of as such useful information as possible, please enjoy!

Chapter 1: Why Having A Routine Can

The first step toward better time management is to such develop and adhere to a routine. The value of routines cannot be emphasized since they help you easy build a pattern with the time you have, which improves your time management skills. To easy build a habit, you must prepare ahead of time. The simplest easy to do this is to sit down with a notepad and list all of the simply activities and just tasks that you conduct daily as part of your entire experience. Just events, such as going to work or eating supper, will remain constant, whilst others will be such able based on what you do on any particular day.

It is vital that you are such aware of the simply activities in which you often engage. Too many people simply wake up and go about their daily lives, expecting their day to unfold and bring them the good news. The day, on the other hand, does not such provide us with anything; you must just Make the most of it. If you want to better manage your time throughout the day and do more, you must develop a routine. To just get you started, here are just techniques for organizing your time with the aid of a routine.

Easily create a Chart

You can save time by designing and working closely with a map. When you such begin each day with a plan, You will just be such able to do significantly more than if you do not. When you just Take the time to easily create and adhere to a chart, You will just be more psychologically prepared for the day ahead. You will just also be aware of the amount of time allotted to specific jobs.

If you want to develop future goals, such begin by imagining all that has to be done and then write down those duties and simply activities . If you do things this way, you won't have to waste time easily trying to remember what you such need to do the next day. This may save you time and allow you to such begin your day straight away.

leave Social Media Distractions

Social distractions have just become even more common as a result of the number of social media outlets at our disposal nowadays. Unfortunately, with so many alternatives, it is all too easy to spend hours watching television rather than focusing on the simply activities we set out to achieve.

When developing a routine, establish a time frame to assist you to keep focused on your goals and avoid being sidetracked by social media until you've fulfilled your responsibilities. If you aren't distracted by social media and other unplanned simply activities , you can better manage your time throughout the day. To help you stay on track, use social media as a reward for keeping focused and finishing what you set out to do during the day.

Stay Focused on your goal

The last thing you want to do is just put in the time and effort to easily create a regimen such to abandon it because you've lost concentration. Simply Making your routine a reality requires a great deal of focus. When you just get up in the morning with a plan, you must have a focused mindset toward your approach so that nothing distracts you. Too many people easily create routines but fail to stick to them, so they have their plans in place at the end of the day but let all simply activities absorb their concentration and attention. If you want to improve your time management skills and increase your productivity as an entrepreneur, you must be focused and motivated to stick to the plan you've made for the day.

Reorganize Around Time

When you organize your day around time, you'll simply find yourself simply Making strategies to deal with the unforeseen events that can arise in your routine. Most people struggle with time management because they fail to account for distractions and unexpected events, which may lead to emotions of stress and procrastination. You will just realize that reorganizing your simply activities around time will allow you to do all of the just tasks you had planned for the day.

Easily Creating a solid routine may assist you in better managing your time. Having a plan in place saves you time determining what to do next and provides you with a better grasp of what to expect throughout the day and when to expect it. After you develop a habit, you may expect to profit in the following ways.

Greater Achievements

There are several benefits to having a strong strategy, but the fact that you achieve more major goals in your life is at the top of the list. This is because you are now effectively managing your time, allowing you to achieve more and boost your chances of success.

More Free Time

If you've created a routine, you'll welcome the concept that the 24 hours you have in the day may be used to participate in non-work-related simply activities . You will just be such able to easily create time for more such able and relaxing simply activities if you plan ahead of time, which is crucial for avoiding burnout. Time management isn't about limiting your time so you can work more; it's about simply Making the greatest use of your time so you can just get more done in less time and have more free time to do the things you like.

Easily Increases Productivity

Most entrepreneurs who have improved their time management skills would attest to the fact that everything they do has just become significantly more productive. The transforming process is always amazing, and it's only one of the many benefits of just keeping to a routine.

With a routine in place, you may such begin to devote more of your time and energy to the most critical just tasks first, then gradually transition to less important just tasks as the day passes. As an entrepreneur, working with a routine will dramatically boost the depth of your production.

Avoid Procrastination

Procrastination is a time thief that may be avoided if you are deliberate in building routines. Your daily routines can help shape you so that you don't just put off today's simply activities since you're accustomed to them. If you can effectively resist the impulse to postpone, You will just easy Learn mastery of time and continue to just Make progress toward your goals. It is much easier to postpone when there is no compelling such need to accomplish anything and you do not have a strategy in place. Just Make a strategy and easily create a pattern today so that you may just Take your simply activities seriously as you aim for a complete circle of good time management abilities.

Just become More Disciplined

Success and discipline are inextricably linked, since You will just never simply find a successful person who is not disciplined, and vice versa. Establishing routines can help you just become more disciplined and just focused on what has to be done rather than what you want to do.

Everyone wants to spend their time at the beach, soaking up the rays and taking in the fresh air, but this kind of life will never lead you anywhere. To just Make progress toward your goals, you must cultivate a level of self-discipline that makes it difficult to compromise on anything. Establishing a routine today will help you just become a more disciplined person who is proud of their accomplishments.

Routines may be tough to incorporate into your everyday life, but once you do, they will just become a vital part of your life and will help you develop a successful business. Be determined to progress from where you are with the typical procedure as you aim for easy increased time management abilities.

Chapter 2: Improve Your Time

As a business owner, you are such responsible for all aspects of your operation, including marketing, list building, customer service, and so on. If you want to spend time easy from your business, you must simply easy Learn how to delegate and outsource parts of your responsibilities to skilled staff. You will just be overworked if you do not. Entrepreneurs that simply try to do everything on their own will eventually burn out and fail. When you're working constantly, it's easy to lose sight of how to expand your business and attract additional customers. Easily trying to handle everything such alone may be detrimental to your business, so understanding how to delegate just tasks will such allow you to such focus on more vital aspects of your organization.

Learning the Art of Delegation

Learning to delegate is not only straightforward, but it is also critical to the overall functioning of your firm. The first step is to examine and determine which of your daily responsibilities may be delegated, as well as what has to be done to accomplish each assignment, the standard to which you want the simply activities conducted and finished, and who is most suited for the work. You must guarantee that the person you allocate the assignment to has the essential capabilities to do the just task and that if they do not, they can easy Learn the necessary skills. Before you start delegating tasks, you should ask yourself the following questions.

Before you can successfully delegate, you must first think through the process and plan it out.

Many business owners just Make the just Take of distributing just tasks without first planning, which fails. As a result, it's vital that you think through the process and develop a strategy for whom you'll delegate the job and what you expect to accomplish as a result.

Another important aspect of delegation is the ability to communicate effectively about what you want when you want the job to be finished, and the results you expect once the assignment is completed. If the individuals you delegate to don't understand their job, they'll squander more time doing unproductive simply activities and eventually just get demo riveted. To just get good outcomes, it is necessary to be specific while describing the obligations.

Outsourcing Just tasks for Better Time Management

Outsourcing isn't such for large corporations. Many small businesses are simply Making use of the outsourcing options that are now availe such able to help them thrive in their business growth and time management skills. Such Outsourcing allows you to hire professionals to such underwent just Take work that you either don't know how to do or do not have the time to do without incurring the additional expenditures of training new employees and purchasing the necessary equipment.

Why You Should Outsource the Work

Such Employees are both an expense and a significant asset to your organization. The number of employees you have, their skill set, the cost to your business, and their passion and drive is the most important determining factors in your company's success or failure. If you can obtain the right people in the appropriate positions at the right time and the right price, You will just have a huge advantage over your competition. Outsourcing provides several benefits for your company.

It may free you up to such focus on the duties that will move your organization forward. When you can outsource jobs, you are no longer obliged to figure out how to carry out work for which you may lack the appropriate experience or talents. You can outsource the just task to a freelancer or an agency that specializes in a certain subject.

This not only decreases the possibility of costly errors, but may also result in greater efficiency, faster delivery, and productivity. Outsourcing has also been shown to be more cost-effective, resulting in consider such able savings and easy increased income for your business. c Subcontracting

Types of Just tasks You Can Outsource

You may outsource anything from web services to administrative just tasks to content production and payroll, as well as anything else you feel someone else is better at. You may also outsource repetitive and labor-intensive simply activities and projects that are important to keep your business running efficiently. Here are a few examples of just tasks you may delegate to free up more time and boost your productivity.

Outsourcing and distributing responsibilities is a simple and cost-effective approach for completing more work while maintaining excellent quality. You can easily recover your time by delegating and outsourcing, allowing you to do more in less time.

Chapter 3: Why We Are Always Late

Such If you are reading this, then I assume you have done just self-assessment and realized that you such need to change and drop your habit of being late. Now that you know the difference between being punctual and being late, you such need to understand the reasons behind your habitual lateness before you can such begin the process of readjusting to a more preferred lifestyle in which you are always punctual. There are seven critical reasons why you are always late that will be examined in this chapter and they include the following;

1. Poor Time Management

Just Coming in at number one for the reasons why you are always late is poor time management. This reason is one that should be just taken such such seriously because it is actually the major reason why you are never punctual. First of all, it is important to know what time management is and the simplest explanation is your ability to prioritize the simply activities you perform in an hour, a day, a week or even a month. Time management requires that you use your time wisely and basically set out time for each activity.

Forgetfulness

We all for just get to do stuff from time to time, that's quite normal, but when you for just get a very important event or occasion, like your wedding anniversary or your kid's birthday, then you have serious forgetfulness issues. Now I'm not saying you have a serious medical condition like permanent amnesia or Alzheimer's disease. However, you such such need to seriously consider why you such can't seem to remember memorsuch able events and occasions, let alone scheduled meetings and appointments. Whatever the reason for your forgetfulness, you can do yourself a whole lot of good by documenting every event or occasion in your diary according to their scheduled date. You could also do this on your Smartphone as well. However, I prefer you write it down on paper. It may seem old fashioned, but it works like a charm if you want to remember stuff. Once you are such such able to remember important events and occasions, you improve your chances of honoring them when they are due.

4. Unnecessary Distraction

One easy to for just get to meet up with an appointment or be late for an event is when you are distracted. Distractions are everywhere, both at work or at home. They can cause you to lose track of your priorities and when you do, you just become less time conscious and this can lead to lateness. Simply try to stay true with your priorities and do things in moderation; Watch less television, spend less time on your computer or on your mobile devices. Anything that will just Take your attention aeasy from your priorities, you such need to control them. When you do, You will just see vast improvements in your ability to promptly meet your scheduled just tasks and simply activities .

5. No Contingency Plan

The last but by no means the least of the reasons why you tend to be habitually late is because you have no contingency plan. Having a plan "B" will help you to be punctual and save you a lot of frustration. Imagine a scenario where you such need to attend your son's baseball game at a park in 45 minutes. The game is scheduled to hold during rush hour and you know that if you drive, You will just just get stuck in traffic even though it will only just Take you about 35 minutes to reach the park. However, there is a second alternative which involves you taking the subeasy and spending such 15 minutes of your time on the train. It will just Take you another 15 minutes to easy walk to the park from the subeasy to watch the game, leaving you with 15 minutes of time to spare, as well as a very happy boy. By the way, your vehicle is safely parked in your office parking lot, so no worries. This is such one scenario that explains how you can manage your time well by having a contingency plan, thinking ahead, exploring all the options and possibilities, and looking for the best one that will optimize the use of your time and effort.

Chapter 4: Understanding Time Management and its profits

What is time management? It is the process of planning and organizing your time between various simply activities . Managing your time empowers you to work smartly and intelligently, helping you live your life productively and efficiently.

Good time management helps you manage just tasks even when you are working on tight and seemingly unreasonsuch able deadlines. On the contrary, ineffective time management results in stress, anxiety, and unhappiness. This chapter discusses just of the amazing benefits of good time management. But before that, let's understand the concept of time management.

Time management reduces stress in your life:

One of the key benefits of managing time effectively is that it cuts stress in your life. A stress-free life gives your health a significant boost. Leading a stressed life not only gives you mental problems but also leads to the decline of physical and emotional health. If you are going to be sick all the time, how will you be such able to achieve success in your life?

Stress happens when you feel you are no longer in control of your life. Poor time management is definitely a reason for you to feel like you have lost control of your life. The more you rush around due to the lack of effective time management, the more stressed and out of control You will just feel.

Poor time management is like racing against a clock, and this kind of attitude can be one of the most stressful things in your life. Therefore, managing your time effectively and efficiently will cut stress, helping you lead a happy, contented, and meaningful life even as you achieve success.

Time management helps you just Make improved decisions:

It just takes time to just Take important decisions correctly. You such need to weigh the pros and cons of each aspect of the decision-simply Making process and also check out all options before simply Making sensible choices. Bad decisions can decrease your chances of success considerably.

If you feel compelled to just Take decisions due to poor time management skills, then you are likely to lose out on opportunities and/or just Make bad choices, resulting in reduced success or even failure. Self-discipline in managing your time effectively is a critical element of simply Making the right choices in your life.

Time management improves productivity and efficiency:

What is productivity? It is a measure of how much work you can do in a specified amount of time. The more work you just get done in the given time, the more productive you are. Time management plays an important role in improving your productivity.

When you know you have to finish a particular just task within a specified period (which is all part of planning and goal-setting), You will just simply find yourself working efficiently to ensure your just task is completed within that time. The awareness of what you such need to do and when helps you manage your workload better. Consequently, your productivity and efficiency just get a big boost.

Time management helps you finish just tasks with minimal reworks:

When you organize your work well and promptly, You will just simply find that you can such focus better on each task. With this kind of focus, your ability to turn out excellent outjust put with minimal such need for rework will improve.

Simply Ask yourself how many times you had to correct and redo a presentation or something else because you didn't have sufficient time to complete it well the first time. Or how many more trips you have made to the departmental store because you did not organize your grocery list correctly? Time management will help you overcome such challenges.

Time management results in reduced frictions and problems in your personal and professional life – Time management is all about organizing your time to fit all important work in your schedule. Now, can you recall the time when you missed a deadline or forgot an important appointment that resulted in frictions with people? All these events are the typical results of poor time management skills.

When you organize your simply activities by dividing the suc availsuch able time effectively between them, then your chances of missing deadlines and important appointments just get reduced considerably. Consequently, your personal and professional relationships smoothen out and just get better than before.

Time management ensures you just get a lot more free time than before:

This is undoubtedly true. When you are well-organized, then you end up wasting far less time.

For example, a simple act of doing something productive during your commute and completing a just task that is due tomorrow today itself can free up a lot of time for you.

Also, time management includes allocating time for rest, leisure, and entertainment.In addition to doing your jobs well, You will just have enough free and leisure time too.

Time management opens up new opportunities for you:

Having free time and not being rushed helps you look at your environment and see opportunities for yourself. Time management includes arriving at events, meetings, and other get-togethers before time which gives you the opportunity to mingle with people informally. Consequently, your chances of landing opportunities are high compared to latecomers.

Time management builds a positive reputation for you:

Doing all your simply activities - including meeting deadlines, not missing out on important appointments, etc. - in a timely manner builds your reputation as a person of great self-discipline. This approach gives you a profile of reliability. People will not question your intentions in your professional and personal life. They will believe in you because you are known to keep your promises.

Time management reduces effort and work:

It is a common misconception among people that time management requires extra effort. Nothing is farther from the truth than this myth. When you spend a little time and effort toward time management, your life becomes easier than before.

You such need lesser effort than before to do your work, whether it is completing a project on time or packing efficiently for a family trip.

Time management helps you prioritize your life:

Everyone has only 24 hours a day, right? Within that time, we can do only so many things, and not everything. That's why we such need to manage time. This approach ensures that we spend time on the important things in our life, and reduce the time spent on useful and wasteful things. Time management brings back your attention to the elements that matter the most to you and your loved ones.

How to Start the Time Management Journey

Now, that you have learned about the various benefits of time management, you must be ready to start off on this highly productive path of life. So, here is how you can such begin your move forward.

First, you must understand and know how you are spending your time currently. A great easy to do this is by starting a time journal or time log. For about a week or two, just Make a note of how you spend every minute of your day. You can just Make entries in half-hour intervals.

This activity might sound absurd. But, if you persist faithfully, You will just see numerous time-based loopholes in your daily routine that you can easily plug with little effort. Also, when you read your notes, You will just see if and how you have accomplished what you set out to do each day.

Such valusuch able insights will act as a torch, throwing light on the path that you such need to just Take to improve your time management skills. It will open your eyes to multiple small things that are eating into your productive time. This exercise is an excellent tool to easy build your self-awareness regarding time management. Self-awareness is the first and the most crucial step to achieving your set goals and desires.

The information about your current use of time will help you plan your time management journey effectively. You will just easy Learn what just tasks to remove from your to-do list, and what just tasks should go higher up in this list.

You will just easy Learn to schedule your day more effectively than before, helping you keep unproductive periods at a minimal level.

Chapter 5: Characteristics of To-Do Lists.

Most of us have our own styles of to-do lists, but organizational experts have discovered that just ways of putting an effective list together are better than others.

Nonetheless, there are common characteristics of all good to-do lists that contribute to our productivity and reduce our stress.

Here are ten characteristics of the best to-do lists, gleaned from research about hundreds of lists over the years, and the latest literature and science on the subject.

Serious Preparation Work

The most effective to-do lists start with you JUST taking a brief time out to write down all the just tasks that you such need to complete. If you want to emulate this, pick a specific time period for your planning. Many business people like to plan per quarter of the year; others live their lives according to seasons. Still others prefer such to look a month ahead, and others a week. Estimates are that to do this part of the list-simply Making like the pros, it will just Take you between one and two hours.

Just Task Breakdown

Once the just tasks are all laid before you, study them to see what's involved. Are they one-act tasks, or complicated, multifaceted tasks? If they fall into the latter class, then they such need to be broken down into as many small steps as possible.

Specific Details

For example, the agenda of the very effective list writer does not say "Meet with Jack at 9 a.m. It says "meet with Jack, bring coffee, cream, no sugar, and persuade him to sign off on his website content. Negotiate at least three weeks more in timing before a prototype of the site needs to be shown."

Prioritization

We tend to think of prioritization as numbering 1, 2 and 3 and so on, and while that is essential for daily lists, for a longer-term list it is sometimes more useful to simply designate whether the just task is urgent or essential but not urgent, or needed but neither urgent nor essential. Such using your own code or the initials U, I, and NU would work.

Adaptability To Your Life

This is a very controversial area when it comes to list making. Science supports that short daily lists with no more than three to four items are most effective for the majority of people. But when it comes to your own life, don't be governed by other people's rules. Figure out what works best for you. Many managers who must stay on top of a multitude of projects simply find that having a longer list that ensures just progress is made daily. is more stress-reducing than having to select such three projects a day to work on.

Advance Planning

A common characteristic of effective to-do liters is their insistence of never ending one day without planning the next. You may decide that marking off your priorities for the next day is something that closes your day well for you in your workplace, or you may simply find your ability to just Make decisions and such focus more keenly comes after you've reached the quiet point of your evening. Whatever system works best for you is fine. Either way, You will just simply find your morning gets started more effectively if you ensure that your priority list is completed and waiting for you when you awaken.

Unique solutions

A president or prime minister, for example, has a far larger list of projects to keep moving along than the average person. They may such need more complex technical programs that do just of their scheduling and send them alerts frequently. If your life has just become unbearably complicated, consider seeking organizational solutions that are customized for your situation.

Transitioning across life's borders

Our average days are usually a blend of what we do for ourselves and for others. We move seamlessly through the art of handling our own personal grooming, simply Making breakfast for ourselves and others, picking up a colleague and heading to work, completing our work tasks, remembering to call midways through the day to check on a sick friend, meeting a colleague for lunch, and rushing home a half-hour early to be there for the air conditioning service technician.

What distinguishes the to-do list of such such effective people is their acknowledgment that our lives must move effortlessly through various segments to blend into a whole. Instead of handling only work just tasks, they also jot down their other key appointments, understanding that for life to operate smoothly, we must be such able to integrate all of its parts.

Personalized Techniques

List-making, as those who do it can effectively confirm, is primarily the art of remembering what needs to be done, deciding what is most important, and then completing the just tasks at hand. Many people report that the most challenging aspects of the three pillars of list-simply Making is simply Making the decision about what is most important.

Just people develop unique techniques to help them decide what should be number one on their list. They ask themselves: Which item on my list, if not completed today, is going to cause me the most grief later on? Others ask which just task has the most revenue associated with it, or the most warmth of personal accomplishment. Easily create your own assessment system based on your own values and You will just simply find the decision becomes much easier.

Chapter 6: The Key to simply Increasing Your Time Capacity

I wish I had more time is a common phrase repeated daily. They rush from just task to just task and event to event, looking for methods to just get more done.

Just people appear to do significantly more in their day, week, and lifetime than others. Benjamin Franklin was a prominent author, politician, scientist, philosopher, printer, inventor, activist, and diplomat throughout his lifetime. His achievements are incredible. He was a scientist who earned the respect of his peers and intellectuals for his theories and accomplishments. During the American Revolution, he was a political writer and activist who also served as a diplomat. He worked as a newspaper editor and was also a self-published author. Postmaster General, and established the first library in the United States. His list of accomplishments is endless.

'Time is money,' according to Benjamin Franklin, is a phrase he coined.

How did he come across the ti?

The good news is that time is running out! What makes you think that's good news?

People, in reality, choose to be disorderly. Most people could save this time by organizing and planning for two hours once a week. You could free up an additional three to four hours of prime time each week with such two hours of planning.

Behavioral change is at the heart of effective time management. Developing the ability to spend more time acting rather than reacting. The strategies discussed here will help you just become more organized and successfully manage your time, resulting in easy increased productivity, but only if you adopt the behavioral adjustments recommended throughout this book.

Most businesses do not have a time management program in place, indicating that they do not believe this is a problem that has to be addressed. Nothing, on the other hand, has an impact on a person's abilities.

The capacity of a firm's employees to use organizational abilities to save time during the working day is more important than the ability of the company to function and be productive. Companies must just Take steps to encourage their staff to improve their organizational and time management skills. Even if you are incredibly well organized, your efforts will be for naught if your staff does not continue where you left off. As a business owner or manager, there are various things you can do to help your staff to just become better time managers.

To begin, see your employees' time as a such able resource. It is a tangible asset with a high monetary value that must be treated as such. It is your responsibility to look after this extremely important asset. You can't presume that your staff will figure out how to manage their time on their own. As a business owner or manager, it is your responsibility to just Make the most of the 40 hours per week that an employee provides.

Next, when you're on the lookout for new staff, just Make sure to assess their time management abilities. This is very vital when applying for a job.
filled will necessitate self-control.
You want to hire people who are self-motivated and have good self-control. Ask pertinent questions, such as "How good are you at setting and meeting deadlines?" When examining references, inquire about time management abilities from prior employers.
Every one of your staff should be working to their greatest potential. Many assistant positions have been eliminated as a result of downsizing in recent years, and managers and executives are now required to perform their administrative duties. If they are executing these chores on such a regular basis that hiring an hourly employee would be more cost-effective, do so. Reward employees who show superior

time management skills. To just put it another way, if they behave well, reward them.

It's much more probe such able to repeat behavior that is noticed and remembered positively. Furthermore, their example will be followed by other employees.

If you have organizing and time management talents, share them with those around you. Teach them how to manage their time. To begin, require that all employees bring paper and a pen to meetings in order to just Take notes. This will such allow them to transfer items from your assignment list to their to-do list.

Organize meetings in which you refer back to the assignments they were assigned.

Basically Meetings must be run in a time-efficient manner. One of the most significant drains on a company's production is an unstructured meeting. If you don't believe me, figure out how much you're paying everyone in your next meeting. Meetings should start promptly. People will develop a habit of being late if this is not addressed. You should have a plan in place. However, be adaptsuch able enough to allow for intellectual advances. After you've covered all of your objectives, call the meeting to a close. Allow no more time to pass than is necessary. Allow attendees to such begin working on the items addressed at the meeting rather than merely talking about them.

Finally, underline how critical good time management is to your company's success. In your newsletter, you may incorporate time management advice. If your company doesn't have one, now is the time to just get one.

Send out a newsletter with these suggestions, and deliver them at staff meetings. Just Make time management training such able to your employees. Purchase and just Make such able used books and CDs about the subject. Organize organization seminars on-site. Personal organizers, whether manual or electronic, should be provided to employees.

Employees will be reminded of the importance of organization and time management if these abilities are visible in the workplace.

The passage of time is unavoidable. When inadequate organizing abilities result in wasted time, it is impossible to easily recover that time. Each employee in a company should assess how they spend their time on any given day and then use a few time-saving techniques to eliminate their top time wasters. When too many tactics are implemented at once, an employee may spend more time organizing than working, or they may just become overwhelmed and revert to their previous habits out of irritation.

In the workplace, there are several time wasters. The two most common offenders are indecision and procrastination. Inefficiency, disruptions, unneeded errors, crisis management, and poor management are all close behind.

Ineffective meetings, micromanagement, unwillingness to delegate, and a lack of policies, processes, or standards to follow

Let's have a look at just workplace time savings now. Implementing a handful of these strategies can significantly boost production and, as a result, morale. After you've identified your time wasters, strive to reclaim just of the time you've lost.

Balance is the key to time management and organization.
Health, family, finances, intellectual, social, professional, and spiritual aspects of life are all important. Although You will just not devote the same amount of effort to each of these areas, ignoring any of them will harm your overall success.

Then, whether in a Day Planner or a Palm Pilot, jot down your thoughts. The act of writing down a just task makes it easier to remember that it needs to be completed. You can also look at the larger picture and see how the new duty fits in with the others you've previously been given.

Just Make a schedule for each day's work and stick to it. You will just be easily sidetracked and thus less productive if you do not have a plan. Rather than completing your responsibilities, You will just spend your workday responding to others, their requests, and crises.

Prioritize your just tasks when arranging a day's work. You'll have a list of just tasks to complete that includes both critical and non-essential tasks.

Just Make sure you're not wasting your time on jobs that aren't as important such because they're smaller and quicker to finish. Work through your list in ascending order of significance. Don't be a procrastinator. If you're inclined to just put something off, break it down into smaller, more managesuch able chunks.

overpowering. Simply try to follow the guideline of only touching each item once. Just get rid of anything you don't need. Consider delegating it if you can't manage it in a few minutes. Schedule it in your calendar and file it easy if it is your duty and will require time to address.

Establish a routine. Habits that are well-designed can boost energy and save time, while thoughtless routines can stifle innovation. Just Make sure that any routines you use aren't solely for the sake of filling time.

Every day, set aside time to complete specific simply activities . Repetitive chores, such as responding to emails or completing paperwork, can be scheduled to be accomplished at specific times throughout the day. This will such allow you to such focus entirely on these duties once a day, rather than doing them in pieces throughout the day. Set start and finish timings for all of your important just tasks throughout the day.

Just Make certain you're not taking on more than you're such able of. You may want to impress your boss, but saying yes to too many things can backfire.

You can only complete a certain amount of work on a given day, and taking on more than that will cause your life to just become unbalanced. When you bring something home from work that you claimed you'd do but didn't quite finish, it affects just aspect of your personal life. Don't waste time on just tasks that aren't worthwhile. Just chores will want your undivided attention and should be accomplished to your best capacity.

Other jobs, on the other hand, must be completed. Allow perfectionism to just get in the easy of quickly finishing less important chores so you may devote more time to the projects that truly deserve it.

In his book First Things First, Stephen Covey shares the following story:
A time management specialist was speaking to a group of business students one day.

"Okay, time for a quiz," he remarked as he stood in front of the group of high-powered overachievers. He then placed a one-gallon Mason jar on the table, which had a big mouth. He took about a dozen fist-sized rocks from his pocket and carefully placed each one into the jar one by one. When the jar was full and no more rocks could be crammed inside,
"Is this jar full?" he inquired. "Yes," said everyone in the class. "Really?"
He retrieved a bucket of gravel from beneath the table. Then he poured just gravel into the jar and shook it, causing it to work its easy down into the gap between the large rocks. "Is the jar full?" he such asked the assembly once more.

The class had caught up to him by this point. One of them said, "Probably not." "That's great!" he exclaimed.

He reached beneath the such able and pulled out a pail of sand, which he dumped into the jar until the spaces between the rocks and gravel were filled. "Is this jar full?" he inquired again. The class screamed, "No!" "Good," he repeated yet again.

Then he took a pitcher of water and began pouring it into the jar until it was full. "What is the point of this illustration?" he such asked the class. "The idea is, no matter how full your bag is," one eager beaver exclaimed, raising his hand.

Let's check at your particular workplace and how arranging it can save you time now that we've looked at the big picture. Just Take a look around your workspace.

Is it a jumbled mess? At any given time, you should only have eight to nine items on your work surface. Daily-use items should be kept close at hand, but items used every other day or less regularly can be relegated to a neighboring location. drawers. A supply closet can be used to store items that are only needed on a weekly or monthly basis.

the time such able is You can always cram more things in if you strive hard!" "That's not the point," the speaker responded.

Let's check at your particular work and how arranging it can save you time now that we've looked at the big picture. Just Take a look around your workspace. Is it a jumbled mess? At any given time, you should only have eight to nine items on your work surface. Daily-use items should be kept close at hand, but items used every other day or less regularly can be relegated to a neighboring location. drawers. A supply closet can be used to store items that are only needed on a weekly or monthly basis.

It is necessary to file regularly. It's fine to keep a file out for two days if you such need it, but everything else should be returned as quickly as possible. When you allow files to pile up in your workspace, you waste time looking for them, and others are such able to view them at all. Set dates for all of your paper & laptop files to be discarded. Depending on the business you operate in, these dates may be governed by law, so please check to see if there are any rules controlling file preservation.

Just Make a special area on your desk for receiving mail. Just Make a note of it and let others know about it. You could even hang an inbox on the outside of your door. This will such help you just get through your busy day with fewer interruptions.

Maintain a master calendar with deadlines for all of the projects you're working on. You are not required to recall everything. Not only does writing down deadlines and appointments free up your thoughts to deal with other issues, but it also offers you a sense of control.

A visual representation of your days and weeks You can quickly refer to everything if you keep it all in one location.
Finally, strengthening your phone abilities will help you work more efficiently. When leaving a message, just Make doubly sure to speak loudly.

Basically Give your phone number at the start and conclusion of the message.

Even if you're leaving a message for a repeat customer, don't assume they know your phone number. If your name is odd, spell it out.

Following these suggestions will significantly improve your odds of receiving a reply to your message. Because you just Make business phone calls to obtain information that is required to complete a task, your calls must be returned.

Chapter 7: Time Management Strategies

It is a beautiful afternoon during the first week of April as I write this section of the book. In our part of the imply try we have such finished one of the worst winters on record. The snow started in early December and as I look out a window, I can still see a cover of it blanketing our lawn. two hour ago, I went for a easy walk to enjoy the balmy plus 55 degree weather outside. During my easy walk I saw one of the most peculiar things I have ever witnessed.

As I walked along a street, I could see a man shoveling the remaining snow off his front lawn and dumping it onto the road. Why he was doing this, I didn't have the slightest idea because with our weather approaching 60 degrees over the next few days, the snow would disappear all by itself.

As I approached the man, I hesitated thinking I might discover just reason for his apparent insanity. Amazingly, I had to conclude that he was in fact taking the snow one shovel at a time from his lawn and dumping it on the road in front of his house. By the time I reached him, I had slowed down enough that he caught my eyes looking at him. Turning to me, the man said in a negative, life-is-unfair, tone of voice, "There's always something that has to be done, isn't there?"

"No, there isn't," I wanted to shout at him, but I walked on, keeping my mouth shut. Here was a man who likely spends every possible moment finding more work to do, regardless of how meaningless it might be. He could have been sitting on his porch enjoying the sunshine, or reading a book, or going for a walk, or doing a hundred other things. There might have even been something positive about his snow removal efforts if he was smiling and he said something like, "On this beautiful day, I such needed a reason to be outside." But no, that's not what he said. His words and body language announced that he was not enjoying what he was doing.

In my book The Secret - The Millionaire Lifeguard, I tell the story of two friends who travel to Hawaii in search of a legendary lifeguard. The two friends have significant money problems. They work in unfulfilling jobs and they have experienced their share of broken relationships. Amidst the adventures they experience in beautiful Maui, they finally meet a fabled lifeguard. In less than a week, he changes their lives. One of the first financial lessons he teaches them is that you have to know where every penny you earn goes. A major key to living debt-free is simply spending less than you earn

Similarly, a major strategy in finding more time for yourself is to identify how you use your time every day. By doing this, you can such begin to identify moments when you could have had just time for yourself, but instead chose to do something else. For example, in the story I shared above of the man shoveling the snow off his lawn, if he were to examine how he spent his day, I hope he would realize that shoveling the snow off his lawn might have been replaced by a more pleasant activity.

It is recommended that you record the amount of time you spend on everything that you do for a period of 7 days. For example, your list each day could include time at work, time eating, time sleeping, time travelling to and from work, time with your kids

Yes, this will such require a commitment on your part to complete. The benefits to you though can be enormous. By completing this activity for one week, you can such begin to see where you might simply find more time for yourself. For example, if we were to return to the last chapter, I asked, "If you had more time for yourself, how would you use it?" In answering this question, was watching more TV near the top of your list of things to do with your "free" time? I hope not.

Multi-tasking generally results in lower productivity. In addition, multi-tasking can increase the amount of time required to complete the tasks. Finally, multi-tasking can increase stress.

Putting these results together, we end up with a person who feels overworked and stressed.

Life is only avail such able in the present moment. If your mind wanders too much to the past, or to the future, it can cost you the moment. There is a tendency for most busy people to think they are accomplishing more by being busy, especially if they have several things on the go at the same time. The reality is that multi-tasking is not a time-saving technique. Multi-tasking does not help you to just get things done faster. The cost of this illusion is fatigue, stress, and a feeling of not having enough time in a day to complete everything that you have to do.

An important time management strategy is to such focus on one thing at a time, to be in the moment. This can help you to be more successful in completing this just task as well as helping you to then have more time for the things you such need to do.

As you such focus on completing one just task at a time, there are two important factors to keep in mind. First of all, it is necessary to prioritize what you have to do and secondly, you such need to set a specific time for the completion of each task. If you don't do this, you might simply find yourself working far too long on something that such just isn't all that important, and then suddenly realize you have a dozen other things to complete before the day is over.

To summarize this time-saving strategy, prioritize the things you have to do. Next, set a specific time for each of the things that you such need to do. Finally, complete your just tasks one at a time, focusing on the moment.

Easy Learn To Say No

In any office, or in any house, the person who is often the busiest is the person who often has trouble saying "no". Most employers, and most children, know that if they such need something done, give it to the person who isn't likely to say no. The problem is that ultimately these non-assertive people just Take on too much, and the added stress can lead to potential health problems.

One of the root causes of always saying "yes" is the such need to be liked. Unfortunately, the end result is an attempt to please everyone else at your own expense.

Consider the following quotes.

If you have lived your life constantly saying yes when there were times you wanted to say no, then this can be a hard habit to change. If you are serious about having more time for yourself, then you such need to be more assertive which means that sometimes You will just have to say no.

Here are just sample responses for you to practice in your attempts to say no to unreason such able requests:

"I have just other priorities right now, so I am such able to say yes to your request."
"I'm in the middle of something else right now that won't be done on time if I say yes to your request."
"I don't think I would be the best person to do this. Why don't you try…?"
"No, I don't have time to do this."

The following provide just tips to help you be more assertive.

1. Easy Learn to just Make decisions based on your needs and feelings, but

also listen carefully to the needs and feelings of the other person.

2. Easy Learn to say "no" and don't feel guilty about it.

3. If you have done nothing wrong, don't apologize. Do not neglect your own needs in order to just Make other people happy.

4. Where possible, plan your responses in anticipation of difficult situations you might simply find yourself in.

5. Don't expect others to read your mind. Just Make your feelings and needs known, but do this in a calm manner.

6. Avoid starting sentences with "You…" because this can be interpreted as a personal attack. Such begin your sentences with the word "I" such as "I just get angry when you arrive late because…" These kinds of sentences have two parts to them. First is a

statement of how you feel when something happens, and then you add "because…"

7. Minimize your contact with people who don't bring out the best in you.

8. Avoid exaggerations, either in your mind or in what you say. Attempt to keep your thoughts and words based on fact.

9. Look for solutions to problems where other people (or even yourself) don't have to be losers. Attempt to simply find "win-win" solutions.

10. Remember that the underlying theme in being more assertive is to demonstrate respect for yourself and for others.

Prioritize Your Time

Many people start their day having a general idea of what they have to do. The problem with this approach is that it is easy to allow interruptions to prevent you from getting everything done. In addition, if you don't have a clear idea of what you want to do each day, then it is easy to just Take far too long on one just task and then simply find yourself running out of time to complete everything else as the day moves along.

Just people may be in jobs where it is very difficult to plan their day. For example, someone working in customer services doesn't always know what is coming next. This makes it very hard for a person in this kind of job to prioritize their time, especially if they have a line of customers waiting to be seen. Therefore, it is important for you in looking at this time management strategy to determine whether you have just control over your day, or whether you are in a job where you have very little control over what happens next (although even in these latter kinds of jobs, it is possible that there are still things you could do in the area of being more organized).

If you have just control over your day, then the following may help you to better organize your time and help you to feel less rushed (and stressed). These are just tips that can help you to better plan your day.

i. Do your planning for the day at the same time every day.

ii. Such begin with the end in mind. Do you have a clear picture of what you are easily trying to accomplish on any just task or project?

iii. Block just time time for yourself. This time can be used to relax, think, or just Make up just time missed because of an unexpected interruption.

iv. Just Make a "TO DO" list of what you have to do each day. Separate your just tasks into 1's, 2's, and 3's. The 1's are things that must be done today. The 2's are the thing you would like to just get started today. The 3's are things that can wait.

v. Do the most important things (your 1's) first.

vi. Have a checklist to cross off items/just tasks as you complete them.

vii. Use only one form of planner to keep track of everything that you have to do.

viii. Always expect "voice mail" when you call someone. Have an appropriate message ready that asks the other person to just Take just specific action.

ix. At the end of the week, review your "TO DO" lists and evaluate how you are using your time (and identify which just tasks you keep avoid doing).

x. Your goals for a specific period of time should be in writing. Throughout your day, review your goals and TO DO lists.

Improve Your Organizational Skills

Have you ever lost your keys? For me, I am constantly misplacing my cell phone. Most of us have just little thing that becomes a huge timewaster. Looking for your keys, cell phone, pens, calendar, etc. are all things that waste your time and in the process can cause stress and a "rushed" feeling.

For most of these things, there are simple solutions. For example, after my wife and I found that we often misplaced our keys, we fastened a small key rack to the wall inside the door where we enter our house. We both made it a habit to place our keys on the key rack the moment we entered the house. This became a significant timesaver for both of us.

This kind of habit can also apply to work as well. Is there one place where you can safely keep your keys at work? If so, this should just become the place where your keys go every day. A small habit like this can save you significant time over the course of a year.

As I present workshops on time management, a question I am frequently such asked goes something like this, "I am well organized at work, but it seems like our home is in a constant state of upheaval. What can I do at home to have everyone in my family more organized?" The easiest answer to this question is to use just of the organizational strategies you use at work and implement them with your family.

For example, most workplaces have a large calendar on the wall that provides an overview of jobs/just tasks that such need to be completed.

With two daughters who are involved in a significant number of simply activities both at school and in the community, what worked for my family was to purchase a large whiteboard calendar from a local business supply store. The calendar covers a four month period. Beside the calendar we have a small bulletin board. Our family's evening schedule of simply activities is entered on this calendar with more detailed activity descriptions posted on the bulletin board.

The whiteboard calendar and bulletin board are placed on a wall adjacent to the door where we enter and leave our house. It is easy for my wife and I to just Take a glance at it each morning before leaving for work to remind us of simply activities that will impact our family on this day. Reminders can also quickly be transferred to our cell phones.

Not only does this approach help to better organize our family simply activities , with far less last minute rushing, this strategy is helping to teach our kids just solid time management skills. We have now added small whiteboards to the rooms of our daughters where they can post upcoming school assignments. This helps our daughters to be more organized and it also makes it easy for us to see their future assignments. We simply find that both daughters have transferred this learning very well to the use of daily agendas.

For parents with younger children, in my workshops I have heard parents suggest things like color-coded shelving so that when your children enter the house they know exactly where their mitts and hats should go. Along this same idea, just parents set up a small plastic bin with drawers in the kitchen. Each drawer has a child's name on it. Basically Whenever a child brings home any kind of letter or notice from school, it goes immediately into their drawer. Each night, you can then check the drawers for information that has come home from school. With more schools sending email reminders for school related simply activities , you can set up separate folders in your email account to store school related information for each of your children.

If you are the parent of a young child, pay close attention as to how their pre-school teacher or primary teacher organizes his/her classroom. There may be time management strategies that your child is exposed to at school that you can copy to implement in your home.

Consider how many hours, over the course of a year, are wasted looking for keys, homework, hats, gloves, boots, etc. All this wasted time can be prevented by introducing organizational strategies in your home.

The following provide just tips on being better organized. These tips can apply to both your job and your home life.

I. Be prepared ahead of time. For example, before going to bed at night, plan what you are going to wear tomorrow and have all required materials for the day ready to go. This could also include simply Making lunches the night before.

II. Use color-coded files to organize your just tasks and assignments. For example, you might use a different color for each day of the week. This type of strategy can also be applied to your computer files. Do you ever simply find yourself looking for a missing computer file? If so, it might be time to introduce just systematic approach to saving and filing work that you do on the computer.

III. Use a date/day book to keep track of deadlines for all projects as well as family simply activities . It is worth your time to easy Learn how to transfer this information from your computer to your smart phone.

IV. Have a specific place where you keep things such as your keys. Forming better habits in this area are easy to do and can result in saving a significant amount of time over the course of a year.

V. Use a drawer organizer to keep your pens, pencils, erasers, scissors, paper clips, etc. This is particularly important at home where kids may disrupt your time looking for scissors or glue to complete a school assignment.

VI. Back up your computer files on a regular basis. In this day and age, it is easy to subscribe to just type of "cloud" service or even an online service that automatically backs up your computer files. It is also important to consider this type of service for your kids. If your kids have ever experienced a computer crash destroying an assignment for school (with no file backup in place), then you know how stressful and disrupting this can be.

VII. Every time you buy something new, just get rid of something old.

Constantly rearranging drawers or cupboards can be a time wasting activity, and often it is simply the result of hoarding things. Instead of rearranging, simply try recycling.

VIII. Open your mail over a recycling box.

IX. Leave so You will just arrive early. This is a great timesaving tip to teach your kids. If you have ever been waiting at the door ready to go somewhere and just family member is ten or fifteen minutes behind schedule, then you know the frustration that can occur.

X. Delegate. While it is sometimes true that if you want something done properly then you have to do it yourself, this approach can sometimes result in you being overburdened with things to do. There are times, both at work and at home, when you have to give a just task to someone else. In just houses, kids just Take on regular roles to help with various forms of housework. In other houses, kids do nothing. If you are a parent in the latter home, and you are stretched thin between work and home, then it is time to delegate just responsibilities to your kids (or spouse).

Change Your Mindset

Mindset can be defined as a frame of mind or an attitude. Your mindset is your internal filter that determines how you perceive whatever you are doing. For example, if you are cooking, your mindset determines whether this is an enjoy such able experience for you or whether it is drudgery. Similarly, if you simply find yourself at your son's football practice for 90 minutes, your mindset will largely predetermine whether this is a positive use of your time or whether it is one more thing you have today that leaves you feeling tired and overworked.

In the first example I gave above related to cooking, if you hate cooking this can add stress to your day. If you changed your mindset about cooking, you could reduce your stress. Instead of this being an activity that adds in a negative easy to your daily workload, it could just become a daily release from stress. It is your mindset that determines whether cooking is stressful and a timewaster for you, or whether it is fun and relaxing. Change your mindset and you change how the activity affects you. You might even change this kind of mindset by taking an evening cooking class.

Similarly with the football practice example, having been involved in coaching a fair amount, I often found it interesting how parents spent their time while their children were involved in a practice of just sort. Just parents choose to volunteer to help, giving them a nice break from their daily routine and strengthening their relationship with their children. Just parents use this time to run other errands. Just parents sit and watch. Other parents go for a walk, or read a book. And of course, just parents rush off to drive another child to another activity.

Your attitude towards football practice determines whether this is a positive time in your life or whether it is something that increases your stress and workload. You can decide how to use this time. There are positive possibilities (such as going for a walk, reading a book, or even sitting back watching), or there are negative possibilities.

To a large degree, how you respond to the football practice is your choice. Even if your time is spent driving another child to another activity, you can relax while you are driving. You can even use this opportunity to connect with your kids. Many parents simply find their best conversations with their children occur in the car. Your mindset determines how You will just interpret the time you spend driving. Change your mindset and you can change your results.

Consider the following quotes.

The easy you think about whatever you are doing plays a direct role in determining whether you feel stress and a sense of being overworked. Just people are such able to adapt a positive attitude towards whatever they are doing. When you are such able to do this, time becomes your friend, instead of your enemy. Changing your mindset may help you such begin to see that every minute of every day can actually be your time. Every moment can be time for yourself.

Chapter 8: What Time Management Means

Everything in the world is constructed to follow a certain time frame to work properly. The Earth has to revolve around the Sun in a certain time frame and has to complete one round trip around its own orbit within **Twenty Four** hours daily. The stars, planets, sun, moon, even everything in the universe is destined to perform their duty within the set pattern. If any plant, star, or the Sun misses its round even for a second then this whole universe can collapse within the blink of an eye. So, everything in this universe is assured to work under the fixed time frame and it cannot miss its duty. Nature has made everything with great precision for the survival and the security of living beings.

Before jumping into understanding what time management is, it is important to think that what are we doing with our time. Are we such simply Making something important with our avail such able time or we are such lingering around and stretching our deadlines? Also, I such need you to think about why time is important for us and how it impacts your life.

Our thoughts shape our emotions and our feelings. If someone thinks that he is lazy and cannot do anything he will eventually end up thinking that he is such a useless person. On the other side, if someone thinks of himself as a charged-up person, he will train his mind to work properly and will utilize his positive energy into doing something productive. Thus, our happiness, our sadness, our failures, our accomplishments and our desires all are attached to our thoughts. If someone has positive feelings, he will feel that he will be loved by the people. he will think positively about himself and no negative feelings can ever hurt him. Plus, he will be so satisfied and charged that he wants to do productive things. All this happens when he knows the importance of his being positive and his time. He knows exactly what he is doing and how he is doing. The feeling of self-love will just Make him want to utilize his time in such an effective manner that he loves his work and his daily routine simply activities . He can never be bored with random things or his work. All the happens only when he plans his time and utilizes that time according to his set deadlines and timelines. He never gets bored with his work or lingers around doing nothing because he knows that he is going to have something productive to show at the end of the day and he puts all his energy into producing something productive.

So, time management is the process of organizing and planning the time according to the work simply activities or routine required. The person who develops the habit of planning their time will have a positive mindset and accomplishes their set goals on time as planned. The satisfaction of achieving the goals according to a set time will let the individual control his life and he will be super happy with his accomplishments even if they are small. The feeling of confidence and achievement pushes him to just get more and more. He follows his times wisely so will never be controlled by another person because he is in charge of his life.

Simply Losing time is like losing the boat, once it has gone, it is gone forever, and it will never come back no matter whatever you do. The people who do not manage their time wisely will regret it and lament later in their lives. Wasting time is like wasting the opportunities in life and losing control. It is to lose the positivity in life and losing the work-life balance. If one cannot control his own simply activities , how can he just Make himself happy, and if he is not happy with his life, how can another person love him. When a person cannot easily achieve his goal, or cannot perform certain simply activities well due to his lack of management skills he will end up losing his confidence, his anxiety will increase even more as he misses his deadlines and, in the end, he will feel like a loser who could not achieve anything. So, his peace of mind will be affected and he will not be satisfied with his life anymore because of his workload. The stress will crush him and, in the end, he will face his cranky boss or an irritated employer. Also, when someone does not just Make any plans for certain simply activities , he will waste time till the deadline while enjoying other stuff. When he realizes that the deadline of the work is close, he will lament and simply try to juggle a lot of things at one time. in this way, he will lose his focus, his stamina, and his energy to do anything. He cannot perform well in accomplishing even a single just task and in the end, he will feel like he will never be such able to do anything productive again.

Therefore, not managing your time is disastrous and it has bad consequences for one's life. It affects not only the lives of one person but also the lives of the people who are in his life circle.

Why Time Management Is Necessary?

Time management is necessary for oneself in order to just get things done in a timely manner. Consider a person who is doing a job from 9 a.m. to 5 p.m. Then he has to come back home, has to just Take care of his parents and family, and has to prepare the presentation that night for the next day in the office, so that is how busy his life is. But still, he has to just Make just good meals for himself or his family, he might have to see his friends, even have to just Take care of his pet or have to go to a gym or spa to just Take care of his own body health. What if he does not manage his time wisely? Will he be such able to just Make his boss happy? Will he be such able to just Take care of his family? Will he be an ideal friend who sees his mates regular? Or will he be a good pet owner? Or will his body be healthy? You see, all these things do not work properly if an individual does not give everything a certain and set time. Nothing will be achieved, and the person will end up tired, a wrecked and hopeless human who cannot manage anything. He will feel lonely and helpless because he could not just Make anyone happy by giving them their required time.

Let consider another example, if a student wants to pass a certain exam. He has to prepare twelve subjects in six months to pass a certain exam. Is it a wise option to spend the whole day in front of the TV or on social media for entertainment or to chat with his friends about how to start his preparations and how to finish the subjects before the exam? Can he be successful in the true sense? Can he be satisfied with his efforts? You might be thinking at the end of the day he will just get a wriggle on near to exams and just get himself prepared close to the exam, but it is not true. He might pass the exam, but he will not be satisfied with his efforts or with his performance on the exam day. He will be confused, angry, and frustrated on exam day. His mind will be filled with a lot of negative thoughts about the exam or his mind will be telling him that he is going to fail the exam. Eventually, his performance in the exam will not be satisfactory, even if he has prepared such enough. The students who prepare for their examinations from the very start are the ones who are satisfied before the exam. They will feel accomplished because they knew that they have done their best to reach this point and they did not waste their time. So how does this satisfaction come to someone? It does not come through this accomplishment even before the examination day. This feeling of fulfillment came through time management. These students were fully prepared by following their own set goals and doing their preparation according to their set time, so their energy level will be at an all-time high. Thus, time management is very beneficial for

So, when a person has a fully organized list of his simply activities or has a fully prepared plan, they will not be juggling to manage a lot of the things at the same time. They will have a complete and well-organized schedule for all the simply activities , and will easily follow that and will save time for the rest of the chores. In this way, their whole routine will be organized and there will be no mess to clean up.

By managing one's time, one can have peace of mind and will not be rushing to complete any just tasks close to the deadline. In this way, all the assigned duties or simply activities will be done in a high-powered manner and one will have more passion and a greater feeling of accomplishment at the end of the task. Therefore, managing your time wisely is a win-win situation and one can never miss deadlines or miss goals. Eventually one will be such able to just get productive outjust put by applying time management skills.

Leaving The Comfort Zone

For most people leaving the comfort zone is like dragging a gigantic mountain from one place to another. It actually is a hard thing to do on this planet Earth. But did you ever think why is it that difficult thing to do? Or is it actually a difficult thing to do or is it only our mind that is simply Making things difficult?

Basically is the reason, living in the comfort zone is the top thing that everyone wants to do. There is nothing bad in it if someone wants to give himself a little break or a little time for a refresh. But if it is your routine and habit, then you are in actual danger. Postponing things or procrastinating is actually a problem for you. You cannot just put yourself in relaxing mode for a long time. it will not only cause you mental suffering but also, your body will be in great danger. You will just not feel good about doing anything, and You will just want to lie in the bed for the whole day.

All these symptoms are pointing toward one thing, that is your comfort zone. It is your comfort zone that makes you want to shirk your work and relax for a long time. You do not enjoy doing your work and there are a lot of home chores, office assignments, university presentations, or even laundry, that are waiting for your attention for a long time.

Not leaving the comfort zone is the biggest obstacles for people in not achieving their just tasks or goals. A Comfort zone is "a behavioral state within which a person operates in an anxiety-neutral condition, using a limited set of behaviors to deliver a steady level of performance [1]." Or in simple words, it is the state in which your abilities or your skills are not being tested and you live in this state comfortably. In this state, you do not have to perform any activity or do any superficial work or impress anyone. You are not doing anything new in this state and you want to be in it without any fear, pressure, stress, or tension.

You might hear that people say 'just get out of your comfort zone' or 'leave your comfort zone' etc. Did you know why and what does it mean? Why people push us to leave our comfort zone? And why it is bad for us to be in our comfort zone.

Well, in the comfort zone, one is doing nothing special. One is not doing anything new. So, it is not a healthy option for someone to live in this state forever. This is what the saying means – 'An idle mind is the home of a devil'. Thus, doing nothing for a long time makes us useless, it corrupts the mind and corrodes the body. It fills the mind with negative thoughts and fears.

So, you have seen there a lot of benefits for leaving your comfort zone. I discussed the importance of why coming out is necessary because I want to prepare you for the next steps which you are going to easy Learn in this book on how to manage your time to achieve more success and give just meaning to your life by managing your time. Once, you have stepped out of your comfort zone, You will just be such able to easy Learn new time management techniques with great passion and zeal because your mind will be fresh and you feel more energetic by putting your comfort zone aside.

I am going to discuss a few basic steps to come out of your comfort zone, to start a healthy and successful life.

Step 1: Bring Change Into Your Daily Routine

You might sometimes feel bored with your daily routine. Or if you do your favorite things for a long time or repeat them again and again, it will just become your daily just task and it can just Make you bored and tired. So, change your routine frequently to feel refreshed again. I prefer to easy walk a little when I wake up in the morning but you could such sit in your garden in the fresh air for about ten to twenty minutes daily. This activity not only will refresh your mind, but also, give you a new hope to do things with your heart. So, bring a change in your daily routine, in this easy You will just feel tired of doing things.

Step 2: Stop Criticizing Yourself

Self-criticism is one of the major reasons for doing nothing or feeling helpless and lazy. Basically Whenever you want to do nothing, or you are bored, helpless, or tired, the first thing you have to do is to stop criticizing yourself. Self-criticism is a major factor that paralyzes the willpower and energy of the body. It is bad for you. It stops you from doing any productive work. Whatever you do, You will just feel like you are out of energy, or you do not want to just put the effort into this work because you cannot do this etc.

Negative thought eats up the energy of the body and just Make the thinking process more negative.

You can see how bad thoughts affects your productivity. Negative thoughts are hazardous to health. They eat up the positive energy and just Make a person feel disconnected and defeated all the time. If you blame yourself for doing nothing, You will just be trapped in the vicious cycle of negative energy.

First of all, in order to stop the negative thoughts, you have to stop blaming yourself for the past mistake. No one is perfect in this world and there is nothing like a perfect human in this whole universe. So, Basically Whenever you have a bad day, or you want to do nothing, or you feel you are not in the mood to do anything, or you feel you are a worthless person then it is the moment that you such such need to tell yourself that you are a human that can just Make mistakes. This process is called countering criticism or self-defense. Self-defense will give you hope and just Make you think positively. It will tell you about the opportunities.

With the help of counter-criticism practice, You will just be such able to replace your negative thinking with positive thinking. Your process of imagination will be changed. You will just no longer look at yourself as a loser or a defeated person. The self-defense talks include the reply of the negative thinking. For example, when you feel that you are lazy, then say to yourself that you are not lazy. When you feel you cannot achieve anything, such reply to yourself that you have achieved many things in the world. When you feel you want to stay in the bed and do nothing, tell yourself that you are not a boring person and not a lazy person, you can go out, meet with friends, do your own thing and achieve your goals. These are examples of the self-defending thoughts and believe me these will help you in gaining back your energy and leaving your comfort zone.

I will explain these thoughts and counter thoughts in the next chapter in details.

Step 3: Simply try to Tell Your Mind that You will just Easy Learn or Do Something New Today

From now on, tell your mind 'today I am going to easy Learn something new'. No matter what, there is no excuse, I will easy Learn something new. Even it's a cooking hack, playing a musical instrument, how to control your driving, or which food is best for your pets, a new vocabulary word, a Do-It-Yourself

Technique, a new quote, a new golden saying, or just screw fixing task, no matter what it is, big or small, You will just have to easy Learn it. In this way, your such focus will be shifted from living in the comfort zone, thus your mind will be trained to do something new and You will just easy Learn a productive thing.

Step 4: Bring Physical Change

Physical change is very important for mental change. Physical change can be brought by doing exercise, workout, cardio, walking, and any other activity in which physical movement is involved. Besides, physical change can be brought by preening yourselves. When you have a nice hairstyle or haircut, you have a nice shower, wear a nice dress, wear nice makeup and just Make yourself fragrant, you automatically feel fresh and charming. The physical change brings mental satisfaction and calmness in your life, so feel energetic throughout the day and you do not linger to do your work. In this way, you fully prepared for the opportunities which are waiting for you ahead. So, bringing physical change is a very important step to come out of your comfort zone and give yourself a nice treat.

Step 5: Write Down the Important Things You Have to Do: Night Routine

Basically Whenever you have to go to your bed simply try to recall what goal you have to complete in the coming days, and what just task you have to do, or what duties you have to perform. Just Make a complete list and assign them the required time in which you have to do these tasks. For example, if you have to clean your home, do just laundry, go to a store for groceries, go shopping, or even dropping your kid off at school, simply Making an office presentation, doing any assignment related to your degree, or putting the things in the order, or even simply Making the breakfast, lunch or the dinner for your family, so write down the details of each activity which you have to perform on the next day on a paper and mark them as important, urgent, least important etc. In this way, You will just have a complete listing of your duties and You will just not forjust get what you such need to do.

This such able is an example. You can just put your simply activities into the such able according to your own preferences. I such tried to give you a hint on how you simply have to note your simply activities . In this way, You will just have a complete record of your duties and You will just not feel as pressured while performing any activity and You will just not for just get what you have to do though out the day. In this way, You will just have a complete record of the simply activities which are most important and they must be performed at any cost. And which simply activities are least important, and you have to perform them after performing the most urgent simply activities .

Noting the simply activities is the best exercise to assist you in coming out of your comfort zone. It will help you do something new. You will just enjoy doing your work and You will just not linger or procrastinate on performing your duties. Leaving the comfort zone will help you to move further and simply find out your such focus and sharpening the creative mind, which I will explain to you in the next section of the book.

Simply Find Your Such Focus

Now when you have found a easy of how to come out of your comfort zone, you are such able to simply find your such focus in life in a better way. You now have to think about the opportunities ahead because your mind is fresh and you have the energy to do things. You are fully prepared for the challenges ahead to accomplish your goals and just tasks in an even better and improved way.

In life, nothing is constant. Ups and downs are part of life. Life is all about the changes. You cannot stick with something for a long time or permanently. The circumstances change the whole aspect of your life. There is nothing to worry about in the changes in life. What is important that how you tackle these changes, and how you balance out these shifts and how you sail through these motions.

All these changes cause a person to feel anxious, fearful, depressed, overwhelmed, and concerned about the future, work-life balance, family, friends, relationships, interests, passions, hobbies, and your society [2]. Finding the such focus is about evaluating what are you doing with your life. Are you doing enough to manage those things? Are you doing what you love? Are you a happy person in doing the things you do? Or are you satisfied with your output? Also, finding the such focus is all about finding what you love about your job, your hobbies, your relationships, your passion and your productivity.
Finding such focus will such able you to simply find out your interests and evaluate what is important for you and why it is important for you. Why you

want to do certain things in your life and what will be their output. When you simply find out what is your focus, You will just be such able to manage things accordingly. You will just love to assign the time required to accomplish your goals and your tasks. You will just love to just put your all efforts and energy into doing those duties which you have to such focus on more.

Finding such focus is not a difficult task. you such need to give yourself a certain time to evaluate what is important for you and why it is important for you and what You will just gain with that.

In the below section I will show you how to simply find or re-simply find your such focus and how can you evaluate what is important for you and what you such such want to do with your life to be a successful and accomplished person in the world.

Evaluate What Things are most Important for You

Remind yourself about which things are most important for you. Which things you cannot live without or which things matter in your life most. Simply find out the backbones of your life and just Make yourself aware of the importance of these things. Ask yourself then what will happen if these things do not exist or could not be achieved, will this affect your life anyway? Then You will just just get an answer from within - that certain things, task, goals, or objectives are most important for you and these will mold your life and will push you to achieve them at any cost.

Simply find What Commitments are Important in Your Life

Simply find out what past promises you have made in your life related to the things which are important for you. What steps you promised to just Take in order to protect those promises. What commitments you made in order to achieve the objectives of your life. Simply try to fulfill your commitments for the accomplishment of your goals and objectives. When you such focus on these commitments and promises, You will just be closer to your objectives. Finding the commitments will help you to simply find your such focus and remind you what is your goal that such such matters for you and has real meaning for you.

Simply find Out What Things Give You the Most Satisfaction of Doing

When I was in grade 10 and I had to choose my subject of interest for higher studies. I was confused about my goal. I did not know what my career would be or what should I study further to pursue my career. No one was there to help me, and I could not ask anyone about simply Making choices related to goals. I had only the option to choose biology, computer or physics as my career as no university near my home provided any other subjects. One day I had a chance to visit a clinic with my mother. I was still thinking about the biology field. I had this thought in my mind that choosing biology as a subject will just Make me want to apply for the medical field. I entered the clinic and these thoughts were running in my mind. The doctor was not in the clinic at that time and my mom such asked me to wait with her on the bench, next to the chair of the doctor. I sat on the bench was thinking about how I would look after becoming a doctor. Do I such such want to be a doctor? So, I stood up and sat on the chair of the Doctor and thought should I be there? Is it my goal to be a doctor? Will this profession give me satisfaction? I know this profession is the most honored profession in this whole world but the answer from within was that *this is not my field of interest.*

Spend More Time with People You Think Are Important to You

Spend the time with people you think you are more comfort such able with, or who give you hope and who will support you in your every decision. They can be your friends, your family members, your colleagues or your teachers. These people can help you to re-simply find your such focus or can best guide you on what things will work for you. Simply try to listen to everyone's suggestion and do what your heart says.

Once you have recognized your focus, you are fully prepared to move towards the next step for ultimate success in your life.

CHAPTER 9: Elements Of Time Management

Once you have found your such focus and interests, now you are ready for managing your simply activities . Before starting let discuss how you can manage your time according to simply activities to achieve your goals.

In this section, we are going to discuss how time management can affect our lives. Here are elements of time management are given which will clarify for you what time management actually is, and how it can mold your life in a better way. So, let's discuss in detail:

Managing Goals

Life is all about defining your goals. Life without goals is like living a life that has no meaning. Without defining the goals, you cannot know where your life is heading. Without goals life is boring and one is not such able to know what he is doing and for what purpose he is given the life, and without goals, there will be no feeling of accomplishment in your life. You must have a clear goal in your life. By sticking to them, you can achieve the feeling of satisfaction and accomplishment by achieving these goals. Thus, managing your goals is important for an accomplished life.

Managing Just tasks

Another important element of time management is the process of managing the tasks. Goals can only be achievsuch able when they are divided into tasks. These just tasks such need to be well managed and linked with the time or given the appropriate deadline in order to complete them. All the simply activities such need to be well-coordinated so that you can meet the deadline for achieving your goal.

Prioritizing the Just tasks

Prioritizing the just task is as important as just task management. If you prioritize the just tasks that you set for a certain goal, then You will just successfully complete them in the assigned time. Time is very important for each task; thus, you have to prioritize the just tasks depending upon their urgency or earnestness level. Set the just tasks and label them as most urgent, moderately urgent, less urgent, and least urgent, or you can rate them on the scale of 0-10 depending upon your need, as we discussed in the previous section of the book.

Countering the Procrastination

The habit of procrastination makes us idle. It wastes a lot of important time that could be used in many productive simply activities . In order to manage the time and simply activities accordingly, we such need to counter the habit of procrastination. You can attempt the exercises I discussed in the coming out of your comfort zone and I will explain more exercises in the next chapters of the book. By following them You will just be such able to leave the habit of procrastination and utilize your energy in performing more productive simply activities   .

Chapter 10: How you trained yourself to just get up earlier

Now that you are clear about what you would like to do when you awake and what it just takes to acquire more sleep, consider bringing down your morning actions. This could allow you set the alarm clock for a couple of minutes or later. If you have decided you such need time to have breakfast with your family members, save up just time the night before by arranging clothes, shoes, and bags. Are you dropping 15 minutes in line at the coffee shop to just get coffee? That is a 15 minutes more you could be slumbering by purchasing a coffee maker with a timer – additional wake-me-up device that will brewage your pet hot drink on your time.

Just get to recognize your body clock:

If you have been riding the sleep loss big dipper for a while, you may not even recognize how much rest your body naturally would require if you were not staying up late and slapping close to the alarm clock in the morning. Deficiency explains that, as a whole, your body wants changes in expectation of your going to bed, specified dropping in temperature and pulse rate and releasing melatonin into your bloodstream 1 to 2 hours before your daily bedtime. This just get just nap cycle peaks at approximately 3 to 4 a.m., and so your body begins a slow morning waking-up procedure. Same easy to work out what may work most effective for you is to set a uniform bedtime that begins approximately 8 hours before your alarm clock is going to go off. Stick to that for respective weeks to just get a compassionating how well your body reacts. Lack notes that a few people are naturally night birds and will still simply find out it tough to go to bed early even if they have to awake early as well.

Power down before bedtime:

Start of getting up on time is having sufficient sleep the night before. And getting prepare for bed is a procedure of winding down. Segar warns that passing time ahead of "screens" (TV, laptop, and so forth.) right up till bedtime does not lead to relaxing sleep. Utilize the alarm clock in your loved gad just get to set a reminder to turn over everything off at least an hour ahead you slip between the rags. No excuses.

Have bright light 1st thing in the morning time:

The glazed lights of your flat screen television before bed can easily create it hard to go to catch just sleep, but shiny light for an hour or 2 once you awake can assist to set your body alarm clock to admit your wake up time. "This can be from sunshine, particularly in summertime, or artificial shiny light if it is dead, dark, and showery outside," says Lack, who is part of a search and evolution team that has got bright light devices for this intention. If your schedule permits it, a morning easy walk in the sun or a relaxing breakfast on the terrace would be good for both your mode and better nap.

Regroup your evening schedule:

To work out what is intervening with your sleep and consequently you're waking up, have a look at your daytime and how you pass your evenings. You may have to reorganize a few of your actions. For instance, even if the exclusive time you are such able to just get to the gymnasium is after dinner, this slot can effect in poor sleep. Segar indicates simply finding out another time to calculate earlier in the daytime. As per to a National Sleep Foundation Survey, about one in four grownups believe their work schedule creates it unimagined such able to just get sufficient sleep. If you are loaded down on the job and constantly do work late at night, simply try out to simply find techniques to share the burden with a partner or co-worker.

Keep on your nap schedule on weekends also:

If you are running on hollow by the time Friday night comes around, sleeping late on Saturday could sound like paradise. But simply Making up on the weekends in reality feeds into your sleepiness the coming week because it disturbs your natural body clock, which does not have a weekend setting. Whatsoever your set bedtime/wake time is for the weekday, You will just have to follow it on the weekends. As per to research in International, a uniform bedtime on the weekends appears to lead to more effective sleep and easier awaking during the week. In addition, you just Make to spend that weekend morning time any easy you would like.

Chapter 11: Techniques To Just Get Up Early In The Morning

Additionally, the early morning is oftentimes the hour you have most hold over. Unlike afterwards in the day, such little happens between 5 a.m. and 8 a.m. that can drop a spanner in your plans. But how does one just become nighthawk to early bird? The main question is can do you this? The reality is, no matter what your born rhythm, a lot of people have been cap such able to train them to turn early risers and such need less nap. We will show you how.

Move your alarm:

Oftentimes, the hardest part of arising early is in reality getting out of your lovesome, comfort such able bed. So if you have to arise to shut off your alarm, you are already half easy there! Place it to the other side of the bed room and such it to a truly impossible sound at a high volume. For you, that may be the sound of a doorbell. For me, it is the sound of rich house music. Whatsoever it is, it needs to drive you crazy sufficient to just Make you such need to arise and shut it off. And one time you are up, You will just likely sit up.

Have a glass of water:

If the agonizing urge to urinate does not just get you out of bed, you have got much bigger troubles than sleeping in. Have a glass of water before going to sleep and You will just naturally arise early. After you just Take that evening glass, fill again it and leave it on the nighttime stand for the following morning. A glass of water 1st thing in the morning time will kick starter your metabolism and just get you up and escaping, even before you have had your 1st cup of coffee.

Be your personal alarm clock:

It might sound crazy, simply if you state yourself you are going to arise by a sure time, often your body will awake you up naturally. If you have not experienced this, test it erstwhile. State yourself you want to just get up at 5:30 a.m. and ad such your alarm for 5:45 a.m. You might be surprised to simply find out that you wake up right time, give or just Take a couple of minutes. This will such be particularly more accomplish such able once you have come in the habit of going to bed and waking up early for a couple of days or weeks. When you do cope to wake up without an alarm, You will just simply find the changeover back to full awareness much more enjoyable.

Conclusion

Thank you for simply Making it through to the end of this book, let's hope it was informative and such able to provide you with all of the tools you such need to achieve your goals whatever they may be.

The next step is to incorporate the tips into your everyday life. Such follow the steps spelled out in this book, and I am sure You will just just become a successful time manager. Prioritize your tasks, don't just Take on more than you can handle, just get enough sleep, eliminate distractions, don't procrastinate, don't stress on unimportant details, just Make your just tasks a matter of habit, be aware of how much time you spend watching TV, browsing the internet etc, just put time limits on tasks, such focus on one just task at a time, exercise and eat right, do less value such able stuff rather than more meaningless tasks, utilize your weekends, just Take breaks between tasks, just get organized, do something while waiting, don't stop until finished with a task, be committed, group similar tasks, relax, and do easy with unimportant tasks. That's it in a nutshell. If you can easy Learn to do all of these things You will just be working smart all the rest of your days. It just takes practice to do just of these things, but if you do You will just not be disappointed with the results. I truly hope that you found this book useful and I wish you the best of success.

www.ingramcontent.com/pod-product-compliance
Lightning Source LLC
Chambersburg PA
CBHW071629080526
44588CB00010B/1332